WESTWARD HO!

The Story of the Pioneers

WISCONSIN TERRITORY

IOWA TERRITORY

Council Bluffs

Missouri River

Independence

St. Louis

Mississippi River

REPUBLIC
OF
TEXAS

FLORIDA TERRITORY

GULF OF MEXICO

ATLANTIC OCEAN

Landmark Books® Grades 2 and Up

Meet Abraham Lincoln

Meet Benjamin Franklin

Meet Christopher Columbus

Meet George Washington

Meet Thomas Jefferson

Illustrated

Liberty! How the Revolutionary War Began

The Pilgrims at Plymouth

Westward Ho! The Story of the Pioneers

WESTWARD HO!

The Story of the Pioneers

Lucille Recht Penner ⌐ Illustrated by Bryn Barnard

Landmark Books®

Random House 🏠 New York

To Eli Forrest Koskoff
—L.R.P.

For my mother, who went west
—B.B.

First Landmark Books® edition, 2002.

Text copyright © 1997 by Lucille Recht Penner.

Illustrations copyright © 1997 by Bryn Barnard.

All rights reserved under International and Pan-American Copyright Conventions. Published in the United States by Random House, Inc., New York, and simultaneously in Canada by Random House of Canada Limited, Toronto. Originally published in slightly different form by Random House, Inc., in 1997. Cover art courtesy of Christie's Images/The Bridgeman Art Library.

www.randomhouse.com/kids

Library of Congress Cataloging-in-Publication Data
Penner, Lucille Recht. Westward ho! : the story of the pioneers / by Lucille Recht Penner ; illustrated by Bryn Barnard.
p. cm. — (Landmark books) SUMMARY: Depicts the settlement of the American west during the 1800s.
ISBN 0-679-84776-6 (trade) — ISBN 0-679-94776-0 (lib. bdg.) — ISBN 0-375-82199-6 (pbk.)
1. Pioneers—West (U.S.)—History—Juvenile literature. 2. Overland journeys to the Pacific—Juvenile literature.
3. Frontier and pioneer life—West (U.S.)—Juvenile literature. 4. West (U.S.)—History—Juvenile literature.
[1. Overland journeys to the Pacific. 2. Frontier and pioneer life—West (U.S.). 3. West (U.S.)—History.]
I. Barnard, Bryn, ill. II. Title. III. Series. F596.P457 1997 978—dc21 97-281

Printed in the United States of America July 2002 10 9 8 7 6 5 4 3 2 1

RANDOM HOUSE and colophon and LANDMARK BOOKS and colophon are registered trademarks of Random House, Inc.

CONTENTS

·I·
THE GREAT UNKNOWN

The pioneers—the men, women, and children who settled the American West—were heroes. Their struggle is a story of adventure, daring, and courage.

Leaving home forever, turning their backs on everything familiar, they walked into a dark wilderness.

What lay ahead of them? Dangerous animals and unfamiliar people. Freezing blizzards and scorching deserts. Sickness, loneliness, and fear.

What drove them on? Love of adventure. The search for fertile land. A dream of freedom and equality.

And what could stop them? Almost nothing! One woman

Who were the pioneers? Most of them were from the eastern states. Some came from Europe. Some—such as the Mormons—sought religious freedom. Others were freed or escaped black slaves.

The settlers couldn't carry much along on their difficult journey. Most of their dearest possessions had to be sold or left behind.

staggered across a burning desert, carrying her two children on her back, even though her tongue had turned black and hung out with thirst.

But there was more than hardship—there were many acts of kindness, too. When one band of pioneers, snowbound in the mountains, was threatened with starvation, an Indian left a pile of edible roots for them to find.

When one pioneer baby died, her mother buried her beside the trail and left a note under a stone: "Please take care of my baby's grave." Tired travelers often stopped to place flowers on the little plot.

History is the story of what happened in the past. But it is also the story of today. The pioneers settled the West with a daring and determination that still show us how to live with the "pioneer spirit."

Most pioneers would never return to their old homes. They had to tell their friends and relatives good-bye forever.

In the late 1700s, eager settlers followed the first trail across the Appalachian Mountains. It led through a pass called the Cumberland Gap. Beyond lay what one early explorer called "a second paradise"—a land of juicy wild berries, lush grapevines, fat turkeys, and herds of deer, elk, and moose.

Soon strings of pack-horses were hauling goods across the mountains. The bridle of one horse was tied to the tail of the one in front.

·II·
WESTWARD HO!

Some of the first pioneers simply walked into the wilderness. All they took with them was what they could carry in packs on their backs. They followed faint animal paths through the thick forest.

Inside the forest it was quiet, dark, mysterious, and beautiful. The branches of huge trees formed a green roof overhead. It looked as if no one had ever been there. Indians had traveled this way for hundreds of years, but without disturbing the land.

As the pioneers pushed on, they ate all the food they had brought with them. Now they began gathering nuts and berries. They drank from streams and springs. They hunted wild birds and animals.

Pow! Pow! One or two good shots and there was a pigeon to roast over the fire, or a rabbit to skin and stew in a pot.

On and on they pressed, crossing the Appalachian Mountains. The first travelers on foot were followed by others on horseback. Still others brought along supplies in two-wheeled carts, drawn by teams of horses or mules.

It was much easier to travel on rivers than through forests. Some pioneers built large flatboats with little shelters in the middle to protect them from the weather or Indian attacks. Goods, animals, and even wagons traveled along the rivers on flatboats. For the pioneers, rivers served as highways.

Wagons sometimes splashed through rivers and streams, so they had to be waterproof. Their joints and cracks were frequently painted with hot tar.

Wagon wheels were huge so they could go over big rocks. If a wheel broke, a family might be stranded in the wilderness. So everyone was careful to carry along extra wheels.

The earliest travelers made marks, called blazes, on some of the trees they passed so that people following them would know which way to go. Soon it was easy to see the trampled path. Men with axes cleared trees so wagons could get through more easily.

The first pioneers traveled no more than a few hundred miles. They hauled their belongings through a gap in the Appalachian Mountains. Beyond—in what is now the state of Kentucky—they found rich land, sweet water, and lush grass. Soon the woods rang with the sound of axes as men felled trees to build homes and farms on the new frontier.

·III·
TAMING THE WILDERNESS

After weeks of traveling, the wagons ground to a halt. The weary families had reached their new home.

Often there was no time to build a real house before winter came. So the family built a lean-to called a half-camp. Its back rested against a bank of earth. Its sides and top were built of branches and bark, then slathered with mud and covered with animal skins. Near the half-camp's open front, a huge fire burned night and day. It provided light and heat, and also kept wild animals away.

What was it like to live in a half-camp? Drafty, crowded, dark, smoky, and smelly! Nevertheless, a half-camp was a welcome shelter after the rough journey through the wilderness.

In the early 1800s, pioneers began to settle the prairies of the Midwest. This was a land with no trees for mile after mile. Without any wood, how could they build their houses?

There was little to use but dirt—so they used it. They cut out blocks of prairie sod. Sod was simply earth thickly twined with tangled plant roots.

A house made from blocks of sod was called a soddy. To build it, sod blocks were stacked like bricks and glued together with mud. A soddy stayed cool in summer and warm in winter.

But when it rained, water leaked through the roof. Everyone was always coughing. Mice, gophers, and beetles lived in the cracks between the blocks. Snakes slithered in to eat the mice, then sunned themselves on the doorstep.

Soddies were often dug right into a hillside. After a few months, grass and flowers grew over the roof. The little house looked like part of the hill. Cattle and buffalo sometimes wandered over the roof and fell through—right into the house!

Pioneer families who settled in the woods built log cabins. The first cabins had only one small room.

Building them was hard work. Trees had to be chopped down and cut into logs of equal length. Then the logs were notched at the ends and fitted together to make walls. Windows and doors were cut out with a saw.

Children gathered moss and twigs and stuffed them into the chinks between the logs to keep out rain, snow, and icy winds. The floor was simply earth, stamped down hard. A roof was made of coarse grass tied into bundles called thatch. In stormy weather, it leaked.

There was little furniture in the first log cabins. People just rolled up in animal skins and slept on the floor. These skins were usually full of fleas, but, as George Washington once said, they were nice and warm.

·IV·
DEFENSE!

Captured children were often made to carry their family belongings back to the Indian village where their captors lived.

As the pioneers swarmed westward, they made changes in the landscape. Their cabins and fences dotted land that Indians had roamed for centuries. They shot wild animals and birds that the Indians needed for food. In order to plant fields, they chopped down part of the forest, which was the Indians' home.

Soon the pioneers and the Indians were fighting each other as enemies. Both sides felt angry and afraid. New settlers began organizing themselves into small fighting forces. In order to force Indians off their land or to retaliate for Indian attacks, they sometimes massacred whole villages and burned them to the ground.

The Indians fought back. They often attacked from ambush. It seemed silly to them to fight against a force of well-armed men. Instead, they attacked lonely farms, killing terrified families and setting cabins on fire.

Their raids weren't always successful. Sometimes a family fought them off. If the men were away hunting, women and children would have to defend their home. One brave woman, when she heard Indians on the roof, burned a feather mattress in her fireplace. The

Indians slid down the chimney and were overcome by the fumes. Then she killed them with an ax.

When Indians won, they often scalped and killed both women and men. Female scalps were considered excellent trophies. Children weren't always killed. Sometimes they were adopted into the tribe to replace an Indian child who had died, or a brave who had fallen in battle.

To defend themselves, neighbors began to build forts called stockades. If they had warning of an Indian attack, they moved into their stockade. When the Indians charged, the pioneers blazed away with their rifles.

When pioneer militias attacked their villages, Indian families usually fled or died. They had no defense against the deadly weapons of their enemies. Slowly, they were forced to retreat farther and farther west as the pioneers advanced.

Sometimes the Indians shot flaming arrows at a cabin. When the settlers rushed for water to put out the flames, they were captured and killed.

The early forts were wooden fences with two-story buildings called blockhouses built at the corners. From the top story, men could survey the countryside. They shot at their attackers through slits in the walls.

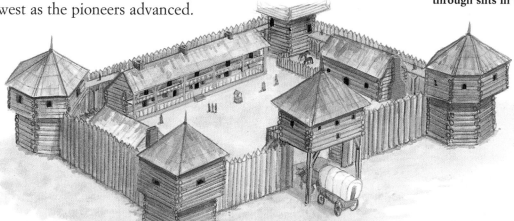

·V·
KINGS OF THE WILD FRONTIER

For many years a tall tree could be seen in Tennessee with these words carved on it:

D. Boon Cilled A. Bar on tree in year 1760

The man who carved these words was a famous explorer and trapper named Daniel Boone.

Daniel was brave, strong, and resourceful. Once he was captured by Shawnee Indians, who made him "run the gauntlet." This meant he had to run between two rows of Indians while they swung at him with sticks.

Daniel zigged and zagged so fast that he almost got away. Suddenly a warrior stepped right in front of him. Daniel put his head down and butted him in the stomach. The warrior fell, and Daniel jumped over him. All the Indians were impressed.

So was their leader, Chief Blackfish, who decided to adopt Daniel. All Daniel's hair was plucked out except for a fringe on the top of his head. He lived and hunted with the Indians until he heard that they were planning to attack Boonesborough, the Kentucky town that he had founded.

Then Daniel escaped and hurried back to Boonesborough to warn his friends and family. He was in time to help them fight off the Indian attack.

Davy Crockett was a great woodsman and a great storyteller. He told many tall tales, and his friends repeated them. One story was meant to show what a great shot Davy was. If he pointed Betsy, his rifle, at a raccoon or a bear—so the story went—the animal would throw up its hands and cry, "Don't shoot, Davy! I surrender!"

Davy was born in Tennessee. He claimed that he had gone to school for only four days in his life, but he was a great student of the outdoors. One winter he killed 105 bears.

When war with the British broke out in 1812, Davy joined the army. Later he ran for Congress. Once, while he was debating his opponent, a flock of guinea hens drowned out the other man's speech. Davy told the audience that their cry, *"Cr-cr-ket,"* was a vote for Crockett.

In 1835, he made his way to Texas. Americans who lived there were fighting for independence from Mexico. Davy joined a group of men who were defending an old mission called the Alamo. Mexican troops attacked and killed them all. Davy died fighting for his friends and his life.

·VI·
PIONEER CHILDREN

JEMIMAH

When Jemimah Boone was a little girl, her family moved to Boonesborough, a town that had been founded by her father, Daniel Boone.

One day a terrifying thing happened. Jemimah and two friends were captured by Shawnee Indians, who decided to take the girls back to their village.

Jemimah said her feet hurt and walked very slowly. Secretly, she dropped twigs and threads from her dress to mark the path. For three days the Indians led the girls deeper and deeper into the forest.

Suddenly a group of men from Boonesborough, led by Daniel Boone, burst out of the woods and rescued the children! They had followed Jemimah's clues.

SUSAN

Although pioneer children worked hard, they found time for mischief. Susan Parrish and her friend Lucy forgot to fill the water buckets one night after their wagon train had made camp. Water would be needed early in the morning to cook breakfast. So after dark the girls took buckets and hurried down to the river.

Suddenly they heard a noise and clutched each other in terror. Someone else was moving around in the dark!

But it was somebody they knew. Through the trees, they glimpsed a boy who was a terrible tease. It was time for revenge! The girls howled and beat the bushes. The terrified boy ran for the wagons screaming, "Help! Indians!"

In the confusion, the girls slipped quietly back into camp.

ANGELINA

Pioneer children faced many dangers. Sometimes they fell out of moving wagons and were crushed under the heavy wheels. Some were killed in buffalo stampedes. Others fell off steep cliffs or drowned in swift rivers.

A little girl named Angelina Smith became so exhausted on the long trip that she could no longer walk. Her mother told her to climb onto a log so she could lift her onto an ox.

But Angelina tumbled off the log and fell onto some deer antlers that were lying nearby. Her mother pulled her free, bandaged her legs, and tied her onto the ox. Angelina had the antler scars for the rest of her life.

JERRY

Children sometimes became very attached to their animals. One pioneer family had an ox named Jerry, who patiently pulled their wagon along the Oregon Trail.

Poor Jerry bellowed and collapsed as they were crossing a desert. The family had to leave him behind and push on to find water.

But when they camped for the night, one of the children grabbed a pail of water, filled her apron with mesquite beans, and hurried back. She found Jerry and gave him water, then twisted his tail to get him to his feet. She coaxed him to follow her back to camp by holding out a few beans at a time.

Pioneer women made clothes for the whole family. When they ran out of cloth, they dried and cured deerskins, cut them into patterns, and punched holes to pull thread through. Deerskin clothing wasn't very comfortable. If it got wet, it dried stiff as a board.

·VII·
WOMEN OF COURAGE

A long wagon train snakes around a high cliff. Whoa! The wagons are stopping. Women run back to the last wagon. Inside, a young woman is giving birth to a baby.

Suddenly a wail rings out. A baby girl has just been born!

A few minutes later, the wagons start up again. The mother and her new baby lie on lumpy bundles and bags of supplies as the wagon bounces along the rocky trail.

It wasn't very comfortable, but this mother was lucky. Some wagon trains never stopped at all except at noon and sundown. Women walked most of the day, keeping an eye on the younger children and carrying the babies.

At other times they drove the oxen while their husbands led the animals along steep, narrow paths or through rushing rivers.

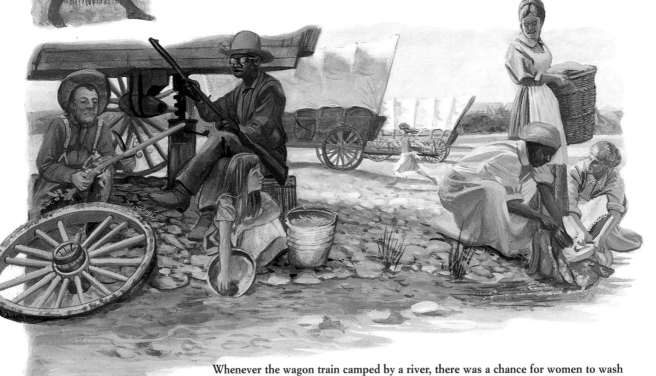

Whenever the wagon train camped by a river, there was a chance for women to wash their families' dirty clothes and linens. But unless the weather was very warm, the clothes didn't have time to dry before the wagons were on the move again. So pioneers sometimes wore wet clothes as they marched along.

Women did the cooking, too. They rolled out dough or churned butter—the bouncing of the wagons actually helped with this—and prepared meals on the wagon seat while their husbands drove.

At night women crouched over small fires to cook the evening meal. Then, by the dim, flickering firelight, they sewed up rips in clothing and in the canvas roofs of their wagons.

And at dawn they were back at work again—building a fire, cooking the morning meal, washing and dressing the children, and helping to load the wagon for another day on the trail.

Few wagon trains had doctors. Women nursed the sick. One popular remedy for measles was a roasted mouse.

Even in the wilderness, women tried to take care of their complexions. They wore sunbonnets in summer and wide-brimmed hats in winter. Sometimes they carried parasols.

CORN FOR BREAKFAST

Salt was precious on the frontier. The pioneers used it to flavor, pickle, and preserve food.

The pioneers gathered wild fruits. At first they didn't like persimmons, which are very bitter unless they are picked at just the right time. Later, Indians taught the settlers to pick them after the first frost. Then they could be made into delicious jams and jellies.

What's for breakfast? Corn.

Lunch? Corn.

Dinner? Corn!

An Indian word for corn means "our life." Corn had been completely unknown in Europe. The earliest settlers might have starved if the Indians hadn't taught them how to grow this nutritious food. Pioneers always took corn seed with them. As soon as they found good land and cleared their fields, they began planting it. Some claimed that they could survive for weeks by eating only two tablespoons of cornmeal mixed with water each day.

Every wagon heading west was crammed with sacks of dried corn and more sacks of cornmeal. Corn was made into mush, porridge, bread, cereal, puddings, and stews. Women made little cornmeal cakes, resembling pancakes, every day. They were very nutritious and could be eaten hot or cold.

Besides corn, the early settlers ate plenty of meat. At first, game was abundant. But as the country became more settled, wild animals grew scarce, and the hunting was not as good. So instead, settlers raised cows, sheep, and hogs to slaughter for meat.

What could you do with a whole huge dead cow after cutting its

throat? The settlers didn't have refrigerators. When an animal was slaughtered, the pioneers quickly ate as much fresh meat as they could swallow. Then they preserved the rest by drying, salting, and smoking it.

Nothing was wasted. After meat was cooked, the bones were cracked for marrow. Fat was saved to make candles, soap, and insect repellent. Hides were cured and made into moccasins.

What did the pioneers drink? Water, milk, and apple cider. Most families brought along apple seeds and planted orchards as soon as they had cleared enough land. Apples were made into cider, as well as apple butter, applesauce, and apple pies.

A pioneer named John Chapman became known as Johnny Appleseed because he traveled west giving seeds and young apple trees to everyone he met. Johnny was said to wear a tin pot for a hat, a coffee sack for a shirt, and no shoes at all!

After corn was planted, children were stationed in the fields with piles of stones to drive away hungry crows.

The pioneers loved turkey meat. To catch wild turkeys, they blew horns made from turkey wings. These horns sounded like the call of a female turkey. When male turkeys came looking for the females, the pioneers shot or trapped them.

·IX·
LEWIS AND CLARK

One dark night, an explorer named Meriwether Lewis sat down beside a campfire to eat his supper—a plate of roasted dog meat. Suddenly a little puppy came flying through the air and almost hit him in the face.

Lewis caught the puppy and threw it back to the Indian—a tall Nez Percé—who was standing over him, glaring. The Nez Percé Indians didn't eat dog meat, and they didn't seem to approve of anyone else's doing so, either.

This strange encounter occurred during a remarkable expedition led by Meriwether Lewis and his friend William Clark, from St. Louis, Missouri, to the Pacific Ocean—and back again. It was a trip through unknown wilderness, into places where few white men had ever been. The expedition lasted more than two years, from 1804 to 1806.

Forty-five men were picked to join the expedition, which was called the Corps of Discovery. They built a large boat, loaded it with supplies and trading goods, and headed up the Missouri River. Clark, who kept a record of the trip, wrote that they saw huge herds of buffalo, deer, elk, and antelope. Once they counted 3,000 buffalo.

The Corps traveled by river whenever they could. If dangerous currents made the rivers impassable, the men built wagon frames and hauled their goods overland.

When the weather got cold, they built a winter camp in what is now North Dakota. There they hired a French Canadian trapper, Toussaint Charbonneau, as a guide and interpreter. During that winter, Charbonneau's Indian wife, Sacagawea, gave birth to a baby.

When the Corps was ready to push on in the spring, Sacagawea strapped the infant on her back and went with them.

Finally, they reached the Rocky Mountains, where they met a band of Shoshone Indians. Cameahwait, their chief, turned out to be Sacagawea's long-lost brother! She hadn't seen him since being kidnapped by another tribe when she was thirteen years old. It was a happy reunion. The Shoshone gave the Corps directions for crossing the Rockies.

They also sold the Corps horses. The men loaded them with their gear and climbed beside them through the mountains. Several horses slipped and tumbled over the icy cliffs to their death, but all the men made it through.

Finally, they reached the Columbia River and floated toward the Pacific Ocean. When at last they stood on the shore, smelling the salt air and watching the huge waves roll in, their hearts rose in triumph. "O the joy," Clark wrote in his journal.

The Corps built a winter camp called Fort Clatsop. They had little food left. Some of the men cut buttons off their coats and traded them to the local Indians for food.

Then, as soon as the weather grew warmer, they started home. The Corps split into two groups in order to explore different routes. Both groups had many hardships and adventures. Some of the horses' feet became so bruised that they needed buffalo-hide shoes, and once Lewis was shot by a nearsighted friend who thought he was an elk. One member of the Corps died of appendicitis during the trip, but everyone else returned safely to St. Louis.

Lewis and Clark's stories of the beautiful country they had explored fired many people's imaginations. Very soon, wagons were setting out on the Oregon Trail, heading west.

Not all pioneers despised the Indians. Jim Beckwourth, the son of a Virginia planter and a black slave, went to live with the Crow Indians. They believed that he was really a Crow who, as a baby, had been stolen by the Cheyennes. The Crows made him one of their chiefs and gave him the name Medicine Calf.

Osceola was a Seminole chief who refused to move to Indian Territory in Oklahoma. He met with a U.S. army general under a flag of truce. But the general had his men grab Osceola and lock him up in Fort Moultrie in South Carolina, where he died.

·X·
TRAIL OF TEARS

Most American pioneers traveled west with joy in their hearts. They were heading for a new, exciting life. But the westward travels of Indians were journeys of defeat and despair.

In 1830, Congress passed the Indian Removal Act. It decreed that when pioneers wanted land where Indians were already living, the government could offer the Indians land farther west in exchange. It was supposed to be a voluntary trade. But many Indians were moved against their will.

One of the saddest episodes of Indian "removal" involved the

Cherokees, who lived in the Southeast. They had built schools, churches, sawmills, farms, and even cotton plantations. They lived quietly. But when gold was discovered on their land, they were told to move.

The Cherokees said the order was illegal. They brought their case to court—and won. But President Andrew Jackson refused to enforce the court decision. Instead, soldiers surrounded the Cherokees' towns, forced helpless families out of their houses at bayonet point, and marched them west to Indian Territory in Oklahoma.

It was a long, hard trip. Thousands of Cherokees died of starvation, disease, and exhaustion. Their route came to be known as the Trail of Tears.

For those who made it to the reservation, life continued to be hard. Proud people were crushed together in poverty and suffering. For them, the trip west was a disaster.

The first horses in America were brought by ship from Europe. Some Indians quickly became excellent riders. They learned to hunt buffalo and even to fight from horseback. This Comanche warrior has his foot hooked over the saddle while his body hangs almost under the horse to protect him as he shoots at an enemy.

For thousands of years, Indian languages were used only for speaking. But in 1821, a Cherokee named Sequoyah invented symbols for writing his language. As soon as his dictionary was published, hundreds of Cherokees began learning to read and write.

Clouds of mosquitoes plagued the travelers. One woman complained that the dough she rolled out was black with them.

Crossing the desert was an ordeal. One group of travelers who had run out of water managed to shoot a stray buffalo. They cut it open and drank the liquid from its stomach. It tasted horrible, but it gave them the strength to go on.

·XI·
PRAIRIE SCHOONERS

Independence, a town on the Missouri frontier, was crowded to bursting each spring with pioneers preparing to travel the Oregon Trail to California and Oregon.

Every day, more and more people arrived. They joined together in wagon trains, elected leaders, and hired scouts to guide them through the wilderness.

In March, the wagon trains began leaving. The spring weather was pleasant. Pioneers rode and walked through meadows filled with wildflowers.

The white canvas roofs of their wagons looked like the sails of ships floating through the tall prairie grass. Soon people began calling the covered wagons "prairie schooners."

Their pace was slow. Most wagons were pulled by oxen—not as fast as horses, but strong and steady. A wagon train could travel ten to fifteen miles a day.

The cry "Keep moving!" was shouted from wagon to wagon. The pace they kept might be a matter of life or death. It was important to cross the mountains before the passes were sealed by snow.

Still, there was one thing the pioneers would stop for: buffalo! If a herd was sighted, men and boys grabbed their rifles and rushed off. With luck, that night everyone would feast on roasted buffalo tongue, considered a great delicacy.

As the pioneers left the plains and headed into the mountains, it became hard to find grass and water. Occasionally, a poor ox became so exhausted and lame that it couldn't continue up the steep trail. Most settlers tried their best to save their animals. Some cried when they had to slaughter an ox that had dropped in its tracks.

At night, the wagons were driven into a circle for protection in case of an Indian attack. Each family dug a small pit and built a fire to cook the evening meal. Sometimes a fiddler played, and people who had walked all day found the strength to dance a few steps before going to sleep.

At sunrise the next morning, they were up and on their way. But no matter how they hurried, by the time they reached the mountain passes the season was already late and cold. Would they be able to get the wagons through before the blinding storms began? Each dawn the cry rang out, "Catch up your teams, boys. Let's go!"

As the trail became more rugged and their oxen grew weaker, the pioneers lightened their load by throwing away many belongings. Soon the wayside was littered with pots, furniture, and even sacks of food.

The feet of oxen grew tender on rocky mountain trails. Some pioneers made shoes for them out of buffalo hide.

People carved messages on buffalo skulls, or even human skulls, and left them beside the path for friends who were coming later.

·XII·
ALONE IN THE WILDERNESS

Snow was falling heavily. Flakes as big as your hand settled on a tiny cabin high in the Sierra Nevada mountains. Only one person was inside—a boy named Moses Schallenberger. Sometimes he talked out loud, just to keep himself company. He was very lonely and very frightened.

Moses' adventure had begun in the spring of 1844, when his family joined a wagon train traveling west on the Oregon Trail. Many wagons had already made the difficult journey. But Moses' wagon train was one of the first to branch off and head for California.

The trail was very faint and rough. When it crossed a desert, the travelers went two days without finding water for themselves or their animals. Then they came to a river that twisted about so much, the trail crossed it ten times in one day.

By the time they reached the mountains, freezing weather had set in. They couldn't pull the heavily loaded wagons up the icy path. What could the group do?

After leaving Moses and the other volunteers behind, the rest of the party labored on. At one point all the wagons had to be hoisted up the face of a cliff.

When snow covered the grass, the poor oxen went hungry. After the wagons halted, they bawled for food all night.

Moses trapped and cooked a coyote. It tasted awful! Although he trapped a few more, he ate them only when he was on the brink of starvation. Instead, he lived on mice, roots, and an occasional fox.

Moses and two of the men volunteered to stay behind. They would guard some of the wagons until the other men returned with fresh oxen in the spring.

Worried, sad families and friends said good-bye. After the others had traveled on, the three volunteers built a little cabin. They were expecting only a foot or two of snow. But the snow didn't stop. Soon the drifts were several feet high. They might be buried alive!

Finally, they decided to try to walk out. After a day of staggering through the snow, Moses was exhausted. He knew he would never make it. If the others stopped to help him, they would probably die, too. So he returned alone to the tiny, snowbound cabin.

For two months, Moses lived all by himself. Later he wrote, "My life was more miserable than I can describe." Luckily, he found some books in the wagons. When he wasn't reading, he was usually searching for something to eat.

Finally, he looked up and saw a figure trudging toward him through the snow. Moses blinked. Then he shouted with joy. His rescuer took him over the pass to California, and a new life with his family and friends.

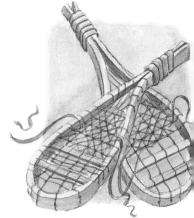

One of Moses' companions made snowshoes out of the hickory strips that had been used to support a wagon roof.

·XIII·
THE DONNER PARTY

Virginia Reed was thirteen years old when she began her journey on the Oregon Trail. She rode alongside the wagons on her frisky pony, Billy. The wagon train captain was a man named George Donner, and this wagon train is remembered as the Donner Party.

Virginia's stepfather, James Reed, was taking his family to California in style. The Reeds had brought three wagons and several servants. Mrs. Reed, who was in poor health, traveled in a huge, two-story wagon with Virginia's younger brothers and sisters.

Soon things began to go wrong. Wagons broke down. Cattle and oxen wandered away or were stolen by Indians. Other animals died of starvation and exhaustion.

The worried travelers began to quarrel—and then to fight. One day, James Reed's oxen became entangled with another man's team. The other man, John Snyder, seized his whip and began to beat Reed's oxen.

When Reed protested, Snyder turned on him. Mrs. Reed tried to separate the two men. But Snyder knocked her down. Then he slashed Reed in the head several times with his whip. At this point, Reed pulled out his hunting knife and stabbed Snyder to death.

The rest of the party was horrified. They accused Reed of murder and sent him away on his horse without his gun or any supplies. This was as good as a death sentence. Without his gun, Reed couldn't hunt for food or defend himself.

But Virginia saved her stepfather's life. On Billy, her pony, she secretly followed his trail, gave him his gun, and then hurried back to the wagon train.

The misfortunes of the Donner Party continued. The wagons struggled on until they reached the spot in the Sierra Nevadas—later named Donner Pass—where Moses Schallenberger had been stranded the year before. But they could go no farther. A storm had sealed the pass shut with many feet of snow.

Some of the party moved into Moses' old cabin. Others built shelters. But they had hardly any food left, and soon all of them were

The Reed children slept in a loft built into the second story of their tall wagon.

starving. In desperation, they chewed on animal bones and hides, twigs, even their own shoes. They ate mice when they could catch them, and finally—as people began to die—they ate the bodies of their dead companions.

Fifteen people tried to walk out. Eight of them died. But the other seven survived and sent back rescuers.

One of the rescuers was James Reed himself. He had made it through the pass just before the big storm. Virginia had saved his life—and now he saved hers. He found all his family alive, and brought them all over the pass to safety in California.

But many other families were not so lucky. Of the eighty-two people who had set out with the Donner Party, forty-seven survived and thirty-five died.

·XIV·
HORSE THIEVES AND CATTLE RUSTLERS

Wild Bill Hickok, a frontier lawman, was a crack shot with a six-gun. He was said to have killed thirty-six men during his career.

Horses' hooves thunder through the woods. Great clouds of dust rise in the air. Men shout and curse. They have caught a horse thief!

Someone runs for a heavy rope. One end is quickly tied in a noose and slipped over the thief's neck. He is forced to climb on top of a box placed under a tall tree. The other end of the rope is tied to a thick branch above him.

Any last words? The thief just spits on the ground. Somebody kicks the box out from under him. The noose tightens, and the thief swings back and forth, his legs kicking in the air. In seconds, he is dead.

This wasn't an unusual scene in pioneer days. People often took

Because he looked young, people called Henry McCarty "Billy the Kid." Billy claimed to have killed twenty-one people. He was captured several times. But he found it easy to slip out of his handcuffs because he had thick wrists and small hands. Billy was finally hunted down and killed by a sheriff in New Mexico.

justice into their own hands. There were very few judges on the frontier.

When bandits sneaked up on a lonely farmhouse and stole the horses and cows, it was a terrible calamity. People quickly rode to alert their neighbors. A group of men galloped after the thieves. If they caught up with them, they often hanged them on the spot.

Finally, the federal government divided the country into areas called circuits. Two judges were appointed to hear cases in each circuit. To visit their entire circuits, judges would spend a whole year riding from town to town. Sometimes lawyers traveled with them. Abraham Lincoln, who became the sixteenth president of the United States, was a traveling circuit court lawyer.

But it took so long for the judges to make their way around their circuits that justice often wouldn't wait. Settlers continued taking justice into their own hands for many years.

Belle Starr's maiden name was Myra Maybelle Shirley. She helped plan many robberies and sold stolen goods. Finally, she married a Cherokee rancher named Sam Starr. Outlaws, such as Jesse James, were welcome to hide out at their ranch.

Bat Masterson was a sheriff, town marshal, and deputy United States marshal. He had a reputation as a great gunman, although he is not known to have actually killed anyone.

29

·XV·
WOMEN ON THE TRAIL

OLIVE OATMAN

When Olive Oatman was twelve, she was kidnapped by Apaches, who made her a slave. But after two years they traded her to the Mohaves in exchange for some blankets. The Mohaves liked Olive. The chief's son married her, and they had two children.

One day, an Indian secretly arranged to sell her back to the whites. He brought her to a riverbank, where he showed her to a group of army officers. As soon as Olive saw the officers, she tried to bury herself in the sand. But when they asked her name, she took a stick and wrote OLIVE OATMAN on the ground.

Her parents were dead, so Olive was sent to live with relatives in Oregon. Later, she married a banker.

ELLEN SMITH

The Smith family—Ellen Smith, her husband, William, and their nine children—joined a wagon train. During the difficult trip, William died.

It was too late to turn back. Ellen struggled on with the children. She tied the three smallest ones onto an ox and drove her sick daughter Louisa in a wagon. The other children walked, carrying whatever they could. One later remembered carrying a blue wooden bucket. Another had the family Bible.

Louisa grew sicker and sicker. Finally, she realized that she was going to die. She begged her mother to bury her six feet deep so the wolves wouldn't eat her bones. And Ellen promised she would.

As soon as Louisa died, the men in the party dug a grave for her. Ellen measured it. It was only four feet deep. But the exhausted men said they wouldn't dig any deeper.

Then Ellen grabbed a shovel herself and jumped into the grave. When the men saw this, they were ashamed and swore to finish the grave themselves. Louisa lay safely buried before the party went on.

MARIE DORION

Marie Dorion, an Indian woman, was married to a frontier guide. She traveled with him wherever he went, along with their two young children. Marie served the group as cook.

One day the men went out hunting. A few hours later, a wounded member of the group staggered into camp. Just before he died, he told Marie that Indians had killed all the other men, including her husband.

Now Marie was alone with her children in the wilderness. She caught two horses, loaded one with food and clothes, and mounted her little family on the other. Winter was too near for her to get away over the mountains. So she found a spring and built a shelter nearby out of bark and twigs. Then she killed the horses, stretched their skins over her shelter, and smoked their meat.

When spring came, Marie packed up the meat that was left, strapped her baby on her back, took her three-year-old son by the hand, and walked across the mountains. On the other side, friendly Indians sheltered her until some other trappers came along.

CLARA BROWN

Clara Brown was born into slavery. She married and had several children, but they were sold and she lost track of them.

When she was in her late fifties, Clara was given her freedom, and she decided to go west. A group of gold prospectors heading for Colorado hired her to cook and wash clothes for them. In return, she received a place in one of their covered wagons.

When the party reached Colorado, Clara opened a laundry. She worked hard, invested her money in land, and became wealthy.

But she still longed to find the family she had lost so many years before. Finally, she returned east to search for them. She didn't find her family, but she brought a wagonload of black people back to Colorado and sent money to help others.

GRIZZLY BEARS AND BUFFALO

After almost all the buffalo were killed, their bones littered the landscape. Settlers gathered the bones in sacks and sold them to make fertilizer.

Hunters made a fortune killing beavers. Beaver hats were highly prized, and a barrel of beaver skins was considered as good as money—or better.

When the pioneers began traveling westward, hundreds of different kinds of animals lived in the forests of North America. Lakes and streams teemed with fish. Huge flocks of birds flew overhead. Herds of elk, deer, and antelope roamed the land.

The pioneers thought these riches would never be used up. But in less than a hundred years, settlers had chopped and hunted and killed so carelessly that many kinds of animals and plants were gone forever.

The pioneers' wagons were too wide for the faint forest trails left by animals and Indians. So they toppled trees and bushes that stood in their way. They crushed delicate plants and flowers under their heavy wagon wheels.

When they chose a homestead, the first thing they did was chop down trees to build their houses and to use for firewood. Soon the forests began to disappear. Animals that had lived in the forest died, since they no longer had places in which to hide, take care of their babies, and find food.

Thousands of grizzly bears once ranged all the way from Mexico to Alaska. Grizzlies grow to be eight feet tall and weigh up to 800 pounds. They almost never lose a fight—except to bullets and steel traps. Today only a few hundred are left.

Once there were even more antelope than buffalo. Antelope were hard to shoot because they ran very fast. But they are curious animals. A hunter sometimes hung his hat on a stick, planted it in the ground, and then hid. Soon antelope came to investigate, making it easy for the hunter to shoot one.

Once there were five billion passenger pigeons in North America. When the pigeons roosted at night, trees often snapped under their weight. Millions of these gentle birds were shot or clubbed to death. The last known passenger pigeon died in 1914, in a cage at the Cincinnati Zoo.

When a buffalo herd stampeded across a deep river, young calves sometimes climbed on the backs of bigger buffalo and rode across.

Fifty million buffalo roamed North America before Europeans arrived. These huge, shaggy beasts lived in enormous herds. Sometimes a herd took two days to pass a particular spot. After the railroad was built, buffalo often forced the trains to stop while they thundered across the tracks. And sometimes steamboats had to stop while thousands of buffalo swam the river.

But hunters slaughtered millions of buffalo for food, hides, and sport, and to put an end to the "nuisance" that held up the trains. By 1889, only about 500 buffalo were left alive in the United States.

What would the pioneers say today if they could see the land that they "conquered"?

Most miners wore red flannel shirts, broad-brimmed felt hats, and high boots. They tucked knives and revolvers into their belts. These were for self-defense. Life in the goldfields was often violent.

Thousands of people traveled to California by ship or wagon train. But some came all by themselves. One man pushed a wheelbarrow full of his belongings all the way across the country—and pushed it home from California loaded with gold dust!

·XVII·
GOLD!

O California,
That's the land for me!
I'm bound for California with
My washbowl on my knee.

In 1848, the first men to find gold in the hills of California, at a place called Sutter's Mill, tried to keep their fantastic discovery a secret. But within a few weeks the news had spread everywhere. The gold rush was on!

Almost overnight, the steady stream of pioneers plodding west swelled to a flood. And not only Americans came. Men left their families behind and rushed to California from every corner of the earth.

In California itself, whole towns were emptied in just a few days. Doctors, lawyers, businessmen, farmers, and even mayors and sheriffs all ran off to the goldfields. Soldiers deserted the army. Sailors left their ships to rot in San Francisco Harbor.

Some who arrived by sea abandoned crates of clothing, food, coffee, and even tobacco along the shore. They were too heavy to carry up into the mountains. And there were no servants left to hire. It was every man for himself.

To dig for gold, you needed only a pick and a shovel. Some men also brought a mule, a blanket, a frying pan, and a change of clothes. Others didn't bother. They curled up right on the damp ground, slept in their only clothes, and ate cold food.

It was a hard life. Miners sweltered in summer and froze in winter. Most ate nothing but bread and salt pork. The goldfields were far from any town, so food was scarce.

Because there was plenty of gold but little food, food prices went sky-high. A barrel of flour cost $400. Onions sold for a dollar each. And the price for a drink was a pinch of gold dust.

Was it worth it? A small number of men got rich. One man is said

to have tripped over a rock, looked again, and realized it was a huge gold nugget.

But few were so lucky. Many came too late. Within a few years, most of the surface gold had been removed. When the miners realized this, many sold their claims to large companies that could bring in mechanized digging equipment. Most went home as poor as they had arrived.

But many others settled in California. Within a few years, a new state was born.

Miners were more interested in digging for gold than in washing their clothes. Women who made their way to the camps could earn a good living as laundresses.

Stories about the California gold strike swept the world. Some Frenchmen packed rakes to take along to the fields. They planned to rake up the gold "leaves" they thought were lying about.

The largest single nugget of gold found in California weighed 195 pounds.

To save weight, letters had to be written on thin paper. They were tied in silk pouches, which were oiled to make them waterproof. Then the pouches were stuffed into the pockets of a leather blanket called a mochila (from a Spanish word meaning "soldier's pack"). The rider flung the mochila over his saddle, jumped on top of it, and set off.

At first, each rider carried a horn. Approaching a station, he blew it loudly. When he arrived, the stationmaster would have a fresh horse saddled and waiting for him. It took him less than two minutes to jump from his horse, grab the mochila, remount, and gallop onward.

·XVIII·
THE PONY EXPRESS

Within a hundred years, pioneers had spread across the vast face of North America. They had survived astonishing hardships to build their new homes.

Now they yearned to keep in touch with loved ones they had left behind. There was already a postal service. But mail took weeks by steamship or stagecoach. When news arrived, it was always old news.

A group of daring businessmen decided to start a rapid mail delivery service: the pony express. They set up relay stations all across the country, where tired horses could be exchanged for fresh ones. They advertised for riders who were lightweight, brave, and handy with a gun.

Eighty men and boys were hired. Their average age was nineteen. Buffalo Bill Cody was only fifteen when he got the job. Another boy was only thirteen! The riders received room, board, and between $100 and $150 a month.

They had to be prepared for anything. Pony express riders galloped at full speed through rivers, over mountains, and across

deserts. They were often in danger of attack by Indians or bandits. They might get lost on the empty plains or in deep forests.

But the men and boys of the pony express were very resourceful. When one rider's horse drowned in a river, he grabbed the mailbag and swam to shore. Then he ran to the next station, leaped on a fresh horse, and galloped on.

Another rider was shot at by a wagon train when he was mistaken for an attacking Indian. He dodged and turned and got away to carry the mail onward.

The pony express began on April 3, 1860, and closed down just eighteen months later. For that short time, the United States was bridged by a band of young riders who embodied the resourceful, adventurous pioneer spirit.

But amazing changes were coming, changes that the pioneers could never have dreamed of. In 1861, the pony express was replaced by an electrical invention—the telegraph. Now messages were flashed instantly across the country.

The heroic riders of the pony express found more ordinary jobs. The gallant horses were put to work pulling carts, or were retired and let out to pasture.

The heroic pioneer era had ended. Modern times had begun.

One rider was ambushed by Indians. An arrow struck him in the mouth, knocking out five teeth and breaking his jaw. But he escaped and got through with the mail!

❧ INDEX ❧

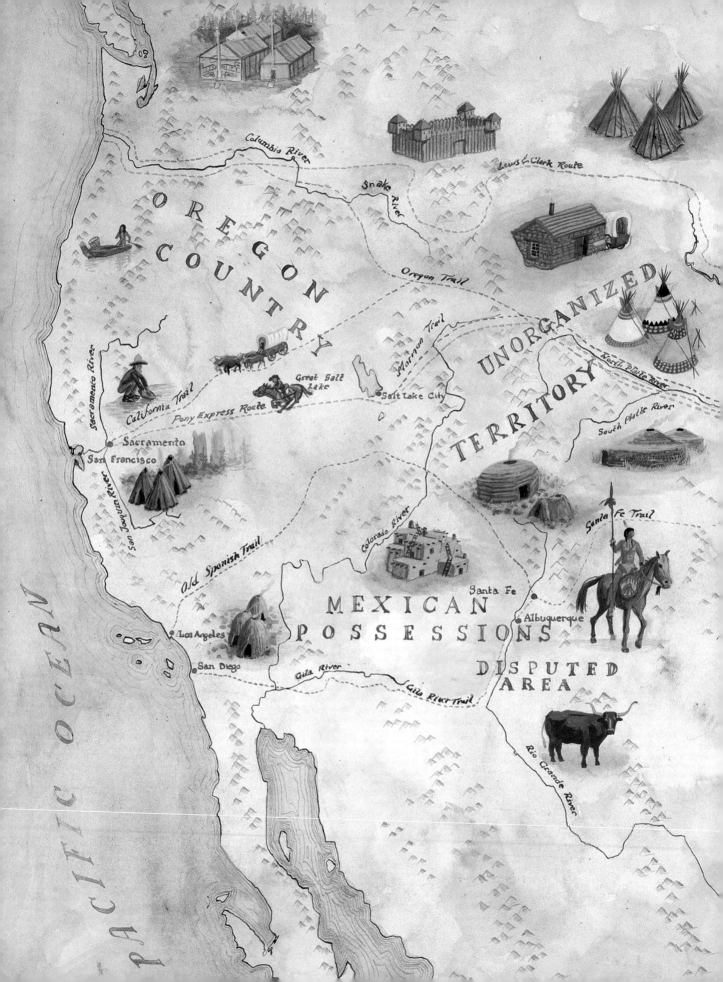

OREGON COUNTRY

UNORGANIZED TERRITORY

MEXICAN POSSESSIONS

DISPUTED AREA

PACIFIC OCEAN

Columbia River

Snake River

Lewis & Clark Route

Oregon Trail

Mormon Trail

Great Salt Lake

Salt Lake City

North Platte River

South Platte River

Sacramento River

California Trail

Pony Express Route

Sacramento

San Francisco

San Joaquin River

Old Spanish Trail

Colorado River

Santa Fe Trail

Santa Fe

Albuquerque

Los Angeles

San Diego

Gila River

Gila River Trail

Rio Grande River